Heartwood

A Collection of Poems

John S. Langley

Copyright © 2023 J. S. Langley

The right of J. S. Langley to be identified as the Author of the Work has been asserted by him in accordance to the Copyrights, Designs and Patents Act 1988.
The Copyright for each poem resides with the author. All images are the property of the author or freely available in the public domain.

First Published in 2023 by LV Publishing

Apart from any use permitted under UK copyright law, this publication may only be reproduced, stored in a retrieval system, or transmitted, in any form, or by any means, with prior permission in writing of the publisher or, in the case of reprographic production, in accordance with the terms of licenses issued by the Copyright Licensing Agency.

All characters and events in this publication, other than those clearly in the public domain, are fictitious and any resemblance to real persons, living or dead, is purely coincidental.

Print ISBN: 978-1-7391381-4-1

Heartwood is the older, central, supporting pillar of the tree. It forms as the tree ages and although non-living (like the Past) it is the hardest timber and is more durable than the surrounding sapwood. It will not decay or lose strength while the outer layers of the tree remain intact.

Made up of a composite of hollow, needlelike cellulose fibers that are bound together by lignin, a kind of chemical glue, it is in many ways as strong as steel and is the most valued part of the tree.

(A piece of Heartwood 12 inches long and 1 inch x 2 inches in cross section, when set vertically, is able to support a weight of twenty tons!)

You cannot have Heartwood without age ... it is an example of the Past giving strength to the Present (and the Future).

John S. Langley

To our sons – Robert, Iain, & Michael, their partners Sophie, Laura, & Kirst, and our grandchildren Abbie, Ben & James who brighten our lives, and to my long-suffering wife, Janet, and to my fortunate brothers Robin & Andrew.

CONTENTS

I. SLIGHTLY PERSONAL   Page

1.	Dear Reader	2
2.	First Memories	4
3.	Want Boxing Day is for...	5
4.	Lessons	6
5.	Super-Sheep	8
6.	Digging	10
7.	Everybody knew him	11
8.	The Chimes	12
9.	Without A Doubt	14
10.	Knowing	16
11.	Telltale Toes	17
12.	Before...	18
13.	Foibles	19
14.	Edinburgh Fringe	20
15.	Ear-wigging at a Book Festival	22
16.	Reflected Light	25
17.	Passing Overhead	26
18.	Morning Walk	28
19.	I saw a Swallow fledge	30
20.	Backpacking	34
21.	The Perseverance of Pheasants	36
22.	In Amongst	37
23.	Unbridled Joy	40
24.	Enough?	42

II. STATE OF PLAY

25.	Negligence (2022)	44
26.	Dispersal	46
27.	An Alliterative Earth-song	48
28.	Our Story	49
29.	Lost Connection - Cocooned	50
30.	If only	52
31.	Good Advice	53
32.	Guests?	54
33.	Best Not to Know	57
34.	Understanding Balance	58
35.	Life's Blood	60
36.	If we don't...	61
37.	The Ship	62
38.	Crow Moon	65
39.	Shopping	66
40.	Fire	68
41.	Embedded in Nature	70
42.	I Got the Science in Me	72

III. THOUGHTS AND THINGS

43.	Dinna Fergit	74
44.	Student Haunt	76
45.	Starlight	78
46.	Home	80
47.	Slow Down	81
48.	Alternative Universe	82
49.	Rainbows	83
50.	The Value of Work	84

51.	And	85
52.	And here was the Fireplace	86
53.	Fire lighting	88
54.	Rain	90
55.	Rainbow Autumn	91
56.	One Among Many	92
57.	Looking Back	94
58.	At the Cave Mouth	95
59.	Worth Remembering	96
60.	What's that you say?	97
61.	The Paying Your Dues Blues	98
62.	Crossings	100
63.	Emergence	101
64.	Belonging	102
65.	Passing Time	103
66.	For the WI	104
67.	Elizabeth	105
68.	Seeing in the Dark	106
69.	Red Squirrel	108
70.	Private Photograph	110

IV. TREES

71.	Casting Shadows	114
72.	In Death	116
73.	Galaxies Collide	118
74.	Sunshine	120
75.	Sequence	122
76.	Skin Deep	128

77.	Differences	130
78.	Leaf Blowing	131
79.	Storm Struck	132
80.	Fallen	134
81.	Rings	136
82.	Utility	138
83.	Green Man	139

V. HADRIAN's WALL 1900

84.	Birdoswald Fort	142
85.	Turret 51a – Piper Sike	144
86.	Turret 51b - Leahill	146
87.	Banks East Turret	148
88.	Lanercost Priory	150

VI. Remember the Best Bits   152

SLIGHTLY PERSONAL

John S. Langley

Dear Reader

Dear reader, how much of self
must I put into a poem
to grab your attention for
more than a moment?

Should I speak of childhood joys
or broken bones or days I
spent surrounded by Nature's
majesty and awe?

Would it make a difference
if it rhymed or has a regular
metre, to keep your mind's eye
focused and enthralled?

Should I tell of my grief that
followed a death or of a birth
that brought hope and tipped
round the cycle one more turn?

Or should I bare my soul for
your inspection, not knowing,
thankfully, of your response
to my utterances?

Heartwood

Would it be better to try
and make you laugh, or to talk
of comfort in Summer Days
the long grass waving?

Dear Reader, tell me what to do
My inner Muse now slumbers
An empty page awaits my pen
What shall I write?

First Memories

I have pre-birth memories… strange, but true. They are memories without words but of the senses. I thought I'd better try and record them before they disappear.

All Sensory …
Warm
(without knowing what warmth is)
Floating underwater
(not needing to come up for air)
Degrees of dark, snakings and shadings of reds
(though the colours are un-named)
Thum… thum… thum
(pulsing sounds, regular, a drumbeat)

The blinding brightness of birth
overloaded with white light
Dazzled
Cold
The wha.. wha… wha… of voices
A cry

How do you explain memories
using language
or the written word
when there were none?

Only a beginning
of sensory awareness…

What Boxing Day is for...

It's the day after
The Turkey is cold
but still makes good sandwiches

Mayonnaise
Cranberry sauce
Sage and onion stuffing

Fresh bread
soft, plastered
with buttery extravagance

In Perfect Proportion!

Pressed down with the palm
Edges checked for overflow
A side of Cheese and Onion crisps
A glass of good White Wine

Mouth open ready...

TIME TO ENJOY!!

John S. Langley

Lessons

There seems to me to be a lot of watchfulness in a cow's eye, more warning than when hands did the work that machinery does now.

When I think back, I remember walking the fields with my Uncle Joe as he cast an expert eye over the condition of his herd

'Nivir git atween a muther an' er calf,' he told me, 'they's viry protective of 'em when they're sucking.' He paused, chewed on a piece of grass, 'an if there's no little uns aboot then alays keep a look out tay see if there's a bull in with 'em. Nasty buggers bulls, best not go anywhere near em.'

I was too young to recognise all his words but the look on his face made his point.

He shook his head. 'George as works fer me 'ad a lucky escape one time. Damn bull was in the byre an George was in there fetching a bucket. Damn thing backed him into a corner a started leaning on 'im, crushing 'im tween its arse an the brick wall. Knocked the wind out of him it did an it would'a seen 'im off if one of t'other lads hadn'ta been close an leaned ovir t'other side an pulled like billy-o on the bloody bull's rope it wis supposedly tied up with. Y'see the rope wiz attached to a ring thru the bull's nose an he wisna happy.'

'He raised 'is 'ead an bellowed 'is discontent, but he moved, that wuz the main thing, he moved jus' a little, jus' enough fer George tay wriggle free an flop ower the wall afore the bull's back legs kicked oot an took a chunk oot a the wall where George 'ad jus' been. Ah ell'ya what, that wiz a lucky day fer George thit wiz.'

My Uncle Joe was a good storyteller but I believed every word.

'Y'kin still see the chunk it knocked oot a that wall. It's not fresh no more mind you, so you's av ter know where e look.'

On other days he took me into the sheds to see the newborn calves and watched smiling as they sucked on my fingers with their toothless mouths, their eyes wide, happy for a scratch on the head, more happy for more food.

Uncle Joe is gone now but I still have his stories and can still see his large frame, his tweed jacket, open shirt, cloth cap and wellingtons as, with shoulders bent, he trudged a steady pace around the farm, his favourite ram's horn headed stick in his hand.

And I still follow his lessons; never get between a cow and her calf and don't mess with bulls!

Super-Sheep

There was wool high in the hedge, clinging to the razor sharp thorns.

'How did a sheep get up there?' I asked.

'Divvn't be se daft,' came the adult answer, 'it's the wind as has blown in up there.'

I nodded in pretended acceptance of this assured answer but in my child-mind, full of folk tales and Superman comics, I saw the field as dusk fell. I saw a sheep look around to make sure no one was watching and then rise up from the ground, stretch out its legs forward and back and fly at low level around the valley, wool from its soft underbelly catching on the hawthorn as it swooped and dived in the joy of flight before returning to its place and settling down again, its secret safe.

'Ah'll tell yer one thing tho,' said my adult, 'sometimes in a morning some a these sheep are in a different field then they wiz when ah left 'em the night afore. I don't know how they does it, if there's a hole or a break in the fence or I don' know whit, then these damn sheep'll find it ah suppose.'

One of the sheep lifted its head from the grass, still chewing, and looked at me.

I winked. I knew how they did it but I wasn't going to tell!

Heartwood

John S. Langley

Digging

The criss-cross sunburn where the vest had been
lay like a chess board across my father's back
a scorched memento of a day spent digging
bending over a shovel, not a spade
important to know the difference

A difference taught and passed on to me
forced to help with the tilling of the earth
under threat of pocket money
that could always be withheld.

I left my shirt on
dripped sweat into the potato furrows
dreamed of finishing and meeting
my mates and maybe even some girls

who all seemed to come from the planet Zog
unfathomable, with smiles that said yes
and eyes that said no. Although I needn't
have worried. The sun burnt my nose
and ruined any chances I might have had.

I blamed my Dad.
The digging could have waited another day
but my seething, wandering, teenage blood
had been dried to a crisp, painted lobster red.

Now I think
I would like to look
at that crisscrossed back again
pick up a shovel ... and get stuck in.

Everybody knew him
(In memory of my Great-Grandfather who, amongst other things, was a milkman in Lossiemouth, Scotland)

And the place was packed
with silence
at the right time

and after
someone laughed
but cut it short
in the middle of a 'Ha'

Do you remember when..
He said...
Memories raised
unsure smiles

and after all had left
and the upturned ground
began naturally
to settle back

a small bird
landed on the cold stone
puffed out its breast
and started to sing

John S. Langley

The Chimes

Listen to the chimes
brass chinking cold
through the holes
in Chinese coins
Gold metal hanging
heavy on thin black cord
swaying in the movement
of the air
the unseen movement
of the air
making music
from the air

Listen to the chimes
the random notes that resound
falling lightly on the ear
echoing through air
that does not seem to move
the unseen air
that does not seem to move
listen to the silent sounds
of chimes
                that only you can hear

Heartwood

John S. Langley

Without A Doubt

There was never any doubt that my father was a Scot.
Born in Lossiemouth he learned to run on the sands
chasing out the tides, being chased home again for his tea.

He was transported south when he was 5 years old
when it was too late, his roots already buried too deep
carrying with him his r's that would always rrroll.

We would go to Dumfries, packed tight in a Morris Minor
to seek out The Bard and a full Scottish breakfast
with oats soaked overnight,his porridge prepared the rright wa

Sport was the worst thing in our house. When Scotland played
England at football, rugby, golf, netball or tiddlywinks...
the resulting score always raising objections

accusations of bribed officials and biased weather.
Neither were we immune to the normal ups and
downs and rode the rough breakers together in the same boat

family-sized, just about keeping it afloat.
At 45 he had his first heart attack shrugging off
help as he climbed the bedroom stairs driven by pride

will power and his own stupidity. Never far from
the Highlands in his head he would say, "You can take
the boy out of Scotland but yer canna tak Scotland oot

Heartwood

o' the man." He had a stroke at 53 and
had to learn to walk and read again. At 72
my mother ferried him North once more not knowing

if it would be for the last time. When they crossed the border
high up on the moors, he said "Stop the car!", and got
out and went and rrolled in his sacred plant: Scottish Heather.

The tough, gnarled underbelly buoyed him up and he
was surrounded by the purple flower bells and powdered
with ochre coloured pollen. Bathed in the earthy,

musky, smells he returned to the car, leaned across, kissed
my mother, and then started to sing
            "You tak the high road ...

Knowing

Unfortunately a university friend of mine called Mike Turner was killed in the Summer break between the first and second year in a freak mid-air glider collision.

A small note, hand written
Signed
pinned to a Notice Board
carried the News
broke the suspense
of wondering
of not knowing

I gazed and read
and re-read
through failing vision
fogged from view
behind a waterfall
of knowing

Wishing not to know
Knowing I could never
Not know
Again

Telltale Toes

By the twitching of her toes
we see the way the real wind blows
She smiles and says that 'All is well,'
but deep inside there rings a bell

that's hardly contained nor contrite
though hidden from the line of sight
churning as the emotion grows
flickering through her twitching toes

Beware! Beware! the calm exterior
you must try to read the deep interior
Don't venture close unless you know
the message of those telltale toes.

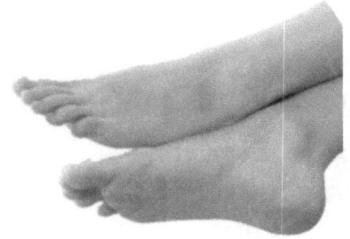

John S. Langley

Before...

This poem was written after reading Seamus Heaney's translation of a part of Virgil's Aeneid and wondering whether we would ever have any grandchildren (we now have three!)

Looking across the river
Faces float
Congeal in the mist
Change agelessly
drift, appear, pass
Eyes closed
White
Ethereal

I see you and my heart jumps
I know it's you
Something tells me
Deep buried
connections
fire, spark
Into life

I close my eyes
You open yours

I hope to meet you
fingers touching
hearts beating

I'll keep my coin

The Ferryman
will have to wait.

Foibles (An Acrostic)

Foibles is such a strange word
One more slight defect
In my character to name
But at least not major, though it
Labels me as not the same.

Everyone has their foibles
So let's revel in the difference

John S. Langley

Edinburgh Fringe

Climbing the hills of Edinburgh
To get to places I've never been
Burning calves as I fight for breath
As the cars pass fuming
The buses pass half-full
And people pass me by

I will make it up these Edinburgh hills
Make it on time for the start of the show
Despite the rain running down my neck
Despite the muscle strain
and the pain in my back
I will make it.

I will struggle through the rain and I will gain
from climbing the hills of Edinburgh
The unforgiving inclines meant for younger legs
Younger legs that pass in droves
intent on speaking to their phones
While I combat the uneven volcanic cobbles
Up which busses wobble
And avoid the cracks
designed to make you topple

Just one more hill to go
I could push on although
There are these shops along the way
That promise hog roast wrapped in fresh bread
And coffee so good it would wake up the dead
Would it hurt just to take a short break?

Heartwood

There really isn't that much at stake
Except the challenge of the hills
Although when I come out
they will still be there

When I'm refreshed
I'll return to the fight
with calves un-cramped
I may even take flight
and what is more
what keeps me going still
Is thinking the way back
must surely be downhill.

A door is standing open
I can see a seat right there
I waddle in towards it
leave behind the sopping air

Please bring on the coffee
bring on the steaming bun
Forget about the prices,
let's remember that this is fun

My companion leans close to ask me
'Are you actually pleased that you came?'
'Yes of course,' I say quickly, 'and I'd do it again.'
(Once I've fully recovered, I say to myself
After all, all this exercise
it's got to be good for my health.)

John S. Langley

Ear-wigging at a Book Festival

The food is foul, the cheese is tasteless

I haven't made them eat couscous
since they were two or three
They didn't like it then
maybe it was the curry sauce
Neither of them will eat couscous
even now
twenty years later.

You can queue here if you like
we're not quite ready yet
or you can go away and come back later
when there are no seats left
and the tent is full of other people
who decided to queue.
It's entirely up to you.

Why do they superheat the coffee?
I can never touch it until it's too cold to drink
or before it's cool enough I have to leave it
because you're not allowed to take food or drink inside.
I can't survive without a coffee.

Where are the toilets?

My seat is in the middle of this row
so of course I arrive last!
Can I get past, I'm sure you don't mind really
Being end of row you must expect it

and by the way my wife/son/daughter
elderly grandmother will be here in a few minutes.
So don't get too comfy

The tickets are so dear now, it must be inflation
I remember when you could...
Buy all your tickets for under a tenner
Have a choice of seats near the front
Chat to the artist about this and that
Not be rushed through the signing queue
Find the toilets easily
... Those were the days...

The staff are nice though
but so young and so busy
I'm sure they get younger every year
I wish I did.

Have you seen the toilets anywhere?

Don't put your face on my trousers
it's covered with ice cream.
Is that raspberry ripple
or is your mouth still bleeding?

His first book was sooo good
What a shame

She's been a much better writer
since she's had cancer and become an addict.

I know where the toilets are if you need them.

John S. Langley

Did you come last year?
Oh, what a shame
it was so much better
This year is quite a disappointment
by comparison
I do hope they get things sorted out
by next year.
Though they never do

Will I come again?
Yes, of course,
I come here every year
I wouldn't miss it for the world...

Reflected Light

My Grandma was like
a gamma ray
bristling with energy

Her grey-haired lightning
crackling
over the soup pan

Simmering with
other people's troubles
Refreshed daily

like the bread
brought back from the
Baker's queue

I feel her warmth
even now
when the Sun has gone

and memory begins to fade

I remember time well spent

Her time well spent

John S. Langley

Passing Overhead

A High pressure system
lies directly overhead.

There is stillness.

The birds chatter
Clear notes travel
through the air

and above
the sky is a cloudless blue
and I believe
I can smell the grass growing.
....

It is the deep sound that I hear first
Like distant thunder
Disturbing the peace

As the volume increases
I look up and see
A passenger jet, possibly a 747
booming overhead
splitting the sky

Pointing forward like an arrow
while disgorging a solid white trail
behind it.

Soon the sound recedes

I can hear the bird calls again
Smell the grass growing

And above
the white line legacy
begins to break.

First into clumps
then dots and dashes
like a message in Morse
that I cannot decipher.

Twisting, it dissipates
into a series of white dots
until only one full stop remains
whose solidity dissolves
into impermanence
a circle of tendrils
whose fingers reach out
seeking
disappearing
until only the blue sky remains
and the birdsong
and the grass growing.

John S. Langley

Morning Walk

Chasing a Robin
down a country lane
Or am I following it?

It waits
until I reach
some magic distance
and then it flits
to a further post

And so it repeats
from post to post
safety to safety
within sight
but out of reach

Sometimes
it sweeps
across the road
into the hedge
on the other side

where it darts
among the thorns
then perches
on an upper
or an outer branch

Heartwood

always pausing
to look back
I like to think
it wants to see
if I'm still there

John S. Langley

I saw a swallow fledge

I saw a swallow fledge
that unique moment

After days and days
wondering if there were
anything
in the nest
a trepidatious movement
a fleeting of black domes

Wide, yellow, gaping mouths
as heads appeared
at the nest's rim
amid the raucous cacophony
caused by the parent's arrival
bringing food

'Feed me…'
'No me…'
'Over here…'
'Feed me…'

Punk haired, black eyed
a pile of poop building
under the nest
as flies are converted
into bone muscle, sinew
colour and feathers

Heartwood

Those barren days of rain
slowed their growth
the risk of abandonment
Dry gaps spawned a new hatch
a new sources of nourishment

Then days of sun
and plenty
and overfilling
overflowing
of growth

a kind of program.
Four chicks quickly out-growing
their mud-made nest
What was too big
Is now too small

Then
on a sunlit morning
sitting on the edge
formed but
still with a wide gape
still with tufts between its feathers

Is it too soon?
It hesitates
Perched there
upon the edge
flexing

waiting for
that unique moment

the frantic beating of new wings
a leaving of the nest
a hovering panic
a de-dusting
a landing on an adjacent ledge

a pause
a look around
surprised
a leaning forward
a head bending
a launch
and out
into its element

pre-destined
pre-designed
prepared to dive
into an unknown fate
To swoop and be held aloft
To climb for the first time upwards
into the sky
scared
euphoric
timely.

I saw a swallow fledge
what a privilege.

Heartwood

John S. Langley

Backpacking

I carry a bag upon my back
Light laden at the first
Though never empty

I've filled it as I've gone along
With mobility first
then language

I've built it up beyond myself
with relationships
of all kinds

Some of the load is light
and easy to carry
as ethereal as smiles

But it has grown heavier
with each step
each new regret

Now memories leak
from worn-out seams
and disappear

Heartwood

I shall carry on
carry the load
as best I can

I may walk more slowly
but I will try not to deny
any of its true content

If strength and mind permit
I shall not fall
nor drop the load

until at the end
I lay it gently down
my journey complete

John S. Langley

The Perseverance of Pheasants

A male pheasant returned to our French windows night after night when the sun was low and turned the glass into a mirror so that he could fight with his own reflection. He could not understand why he could not prevail, why his adversary was so resilient, why he would never give way, never accept his superiority.

A male pheasant fights
with his own reflection
although there is no chance
of ever coming out
on top.

Each day he comes back
to the same spot
fixated on vanquishing
this vexatious version
of himself.

Again and again he comes
each time more depleted
in health and condition
his feathers fractured
his head drooping.

Until the time comes
when he does not return
The instinctual tussle
finally knocked out of him.

In Amongst

November
Hawthorn shed leaves
litter the path
Twisted branches
hung with red haw berries
glisten in a low Sun

Fieldfare
and Redwing
chatter in a mixed flock
Never still, raucous
many voiced arrivals
from colder climes

I walk
the silvered road
disturb a number
that chook-chook
their complaints
and scatter

I stop
in amongst
their number
and stand still
Hunger brings them back
in ones and twos

John S. Langley

Flashing underwing
white and red
as the noise grows
and red berries are precisely picked
nipped
held
then swallowed whole

I am ignored
Surrounded and engulfed
for a while
I join their throng
A silent alien
unable to speak

their language
or understand their lives
I simply watch
and try to absorb
the moment
and hold it tight

The Fieldfare
nods it's grey head
above a mottled breast
and flashes white
as it rises
and cackles away

Heartwood

while the Redwing
with its cream-striped eyebrow
remains a moment longer
to take the last red fruit
gulp it down
then raise its streaked breast

to the heavens
to emit a high-pitched 'seeze'
and departs
with orange-red flagged flanks
taking the breeze
twittering 'I will follow, let me follow'
to the lowering sun

And when they're gone
I walk on
Did it really happen?
The Hawthorn's bare bones
are proof of a kind

Their wing flashes and calls
echo already
in memory

John S. Langley

Unbridled Joy

Inspired by watching our granddaughter at Christmas who had such joy opening her presents - irrespective of what might be inside!

What's this under the Christmas tree
Is this present just for me?
Can I open it, can I please
Was that a yes or did you sneeze?

I can feel my face is smiling
I can see it in your eyes
I can't stop myself from jumping, jumping
This is such a big surprise!

I'll take the wrapping off right now
I like to hear it rip
You don't need to show me how
I've got a real good grip

I'll start it at the corner
I'll tear it all along
Can you hear it grandma?
I'm really very strong

Heartwood

Now it's nearly open
I can peep inside
Ooh I really love it
look at what I've spied

It's just what I've always wanted
but I don't know what it is
Oh thank you, thank you everyone
Wha-hoo, hurray, gee whiz!!

John S. Langley

Enough?

Out of all possible lives I had this one.
Is no-one ever content with their lot ?
The choices made
the people met along the way.

There's no escaping the simple truth
that you enter and leave alone.
But in between you are part
of a larger whole

Whether you like it or not
you could not survive without
the help of others. To clothe, feed
shelter, smile and hold your hand.

So am I content? Of course not !
I would not be human if there were
not regrets and 'what if's'
but I am here and able to write this so ...

   ...maybe that's enough.

STATE OF PLAY

John S. Langley

Negligence (2022)

This poem was printed in the Cumberland News, Letters page on 11/11/22. A fitting day to give thanks for a lifetime of peace within these shores bought by so many million sacrifices. I am sure they did not give their lives in order for us to squander the future of our own descendants. I was battling to come to terms with COP27, our uncertain attendance, our uncertain support, the words of Greta Thunberg and the evidence before our own eyes (the metre used is from a familiar poem written by W.H. Davies in 1911).

What is this world, do we not care
Do we have the right to strip it bare?

Do we believe that there are others
Waiting like expectant mothers?

Look around, in broad daylight,
It's in this Earth we must delight

There is no other, this is ours
It's minutes, seconds fills our hours

When we look at the stars above
We stand upon the thing we love

Can we not see we must protect
Not treat our home with disrespect?

There may still be time for us to use
After all it's only we who'll loose.

A poor place this, if we don't care
and think that we, can strip it bare.

The Cumberland News Friday, November 11, 2022

LETTERS

Time for action

I'M battling to come to terms with COP27, our uncertain support, the words of Greta Thunberg and the evidence before our own eyes. To try and express myself in what I think is a critical time for action I offer the following (using a metre from a familiar poem written by W.H. Davies in 1911)

NEGLIGENCE (2022)
What is this world, do we not care
Do we have the right to strip it bare?
Do we believe that there are others
Waiting like expectant mothers?
Look around, in broad daylight,
It's in this Earth we must delight

There is no other, this is ours
It's minutes, seconds fill our hours
When we look at the stars above
We stand upon the thing we love
Can we not see we must protect
Not treat our home with disrespect?

There may still be time for us to use
After all it's only we who'll lose.
A poor place this, if we don't care
and think that we, can strip it bare.

JOHN S. LANGLEY
Brampton

John S. Langley

Dispersal

During late Summer and Autumn you often see fine silken strands shimmering and drifting in the sunlight from the top of fence posts. These are produced by spiders that need to disperse in order to avoid competition with parents and siblings. Once at the top of the fence posts they point their abdomen into the air and release silk. The silk hardens and more is pulled from them as the wind catches it. Eventually the thread is long enough for the spiderling to be picked up like a kite and carried away to who knows where...

Strung
from the top of fence posts
and out
across the path
gossamer threads
reach
for liftoff

Invisible
until sunlight betrays
their presence
glistening
as the spinning spider
waits

to be taken

to spread
dispersed
at the whim
of unseen currents of air
this fine Autumn day

John S. Langley

An Alliterative Earth-song

Beneath a blanket of breath
wander the wild ones
low light lowing buffalo
stamping silent sods of earth
mountains of mothers and horns

While whales sleep beneath the waves
languorously large levitating upwards
foul air filled to blow and breathe in afresh
amidst white water, skin-wrapped in
barnacles, binging on passing plankton

Above in air an arrow swooping gannet
spears the surface in search of fish
And above the land a barn owl flits
sharp eyes scouring the silent fields
to find a flicker or a twist

Asleep, I dream of doom and dread
my pillowed head held heavy in remorse
for all the things I only see in thought
things I ought to value and protect but
slumber beckons and I do naught...

Our Story

It's the story of our species
that we know how to start
but not how to finish.

Nuclear power
reducing emissions
Nuclear waste
the result of the fission

Coal, Gas and oil
all shedding CO2
Carbon capture can help
but who pays, me or you?

Palm oil to replace animal products
rainforest destruction to create the space
but too far away to pay much notice
and anyway it's no disgrace

Farming and Logging
and Species extinction
Can we not see
the juxtaposition?

Peat bogs are drained
and we're growing tomatoes
Releasing stored gases
One more greenhouse to grow

Yes, we know how to start
but not what to do then
We'd better learn fast
but I wonder when?

John S. Langley

Lost Connection
- Cocooned

Inside a room with windows that look out
Double glazed to let in only light

Inside a house with walls to partition
our lives into suitable compartments

Inside a car with the radio on
concentrating on the Satnav's voice

Inside a bus watching the houses go by
counting the Stops before we get off

Inside a train we breathe to the beat
as the fields flash past quickly
and we count the sheep

Cubicle, Unit, Booth, Nook, Chamber, Cave
Walled, roofed or windowed for energy to save

Reinforcing detachment, our lives lived apart
Our utter acceptance of this as being smart

Heartwood

And we wonder why we've lost
connection with the land
Why Environment sounds like a charity
that we think we should support
if only we had the time
or a little more spare change

Surely there will come a time
when the paradigm is shifted
and we move back towards
what our ancestors already knew
and we have chosen to discard.

I pray it does not come too late...

John S. Langley

If only

If only we could use our cleverness
to work with Nature and not against it.

Would we really achieve much less
if we applied ourselves and used our wits
to appreciate and nurture this Eden
and not rape and pillage and pollute
with no thought of what we've done
and leave it to the future to dispute

This is our own unique home planet
let's not ignore our great good fortune
and destroy our one and only nest
believing it's someone else's portion

Who will make up for our mistakes?
If we could use our cleverness
to work with Nature and not just take
there may be time to fix this mess

Good Advice

"If I was going there, son
I widn't start from here"

My map was creased and torn
with use, with age, with wrong turnings

It had been a winding road that
had lead me here, sometimes

soft underfoot, other times hard
with stones that could turn an ankle

and streams that seemed too wide to cross
"For better or for worse here is where I am,"

I said, "I can't start from anywhere else
even if I wanted to..."

"Aye well, yer'd better just make
the best of it then," he said.

John S. Langley

Guests?

We are the animals, the plants
and insects that were here
before...
    ...the new guest arrived at our door

We let him in and
then another followed
we could not turn her away

They liked what they saw
admired the decor
particularly the curtains
the rugs on the floor

We shared many stories
late into the night
but grew slowly apart
though it didn't seem right

Then they went down
into the basement where
we did not see them for many a year
and almost forgot they were there

Heartwood

Every now and again
we heard voices
and heat rose through the floor
they seemed to be making good choices

We left them alone
thought that things would settle
then there were sounds
the crash and clashing of metal

And when they came up
out of the dark
there were so many of them
and they carried a spark

They brought sharp forged teeth
at the end of a stick
and attacked us
with their new magic

So, though we'd been the hosts
we ran where we could
and why so many of us had to die
we never really understood

John S. Langley

Now we look on in trepidation
see the light inside their windows
and while our outside diminishes
their inside, like an amoeba, grows

covering the fertile earth in hard grey
a solid foundation on which to build
static hard shells to hide in
to protect them from being killed

Their teeth are now the sharpest
their arms reach out so far
their metal is stronger than our bone
there's only one winner of this war

These guests are not now welcome
though they have come to believe
that they are the rightful sole owners
but we wish that they would leave.

Best Not to Know

Are there things that it's best not to know ?
That the Sun will swallow the Earth
That the Universe is growing colder
That we are getting older.

Does all this knowledge help us live?
To just enjoy the time we have
To sit and stare and contemplate
To consider what we each create.

Is too much knowledge a dangerous thing ?
Our endless further search for more
Let's not forget the nearby things
The beauty that each day brings.

Let us amongst the mass of News
of data, debate, or global views
remember that we are only small
and have no right to be here at all.

John S. Langley

Understanding Balance

It's only taken about 5,000 years
for us to upset the balance
and accelerate change against
our own best interests.

At least at the start we could claim
ignorance of the finite nature
of the world whose edges
we were yet to reach.

But as we expanded our domains
we pushed out all the others
that got in our way
as if they did not matter.

Now mass extinctions rage
while we wonder why
ecosystems are collapsing
pollinators decline and

our own food supply dwindles.

Heartwood

Now we seek to artificially redress
the balance in our favour, replacing trees
with carbon removal factories
increased chemicals to grow our crops

Have we not learnt that there is
no permanent balance
only different rates of change ?

That to understand our Eden
is to work within its limits
whilst appreciating its beauty.

In the end
this will be the only thing.

John S. Langley

Life's Blood

As I approached
the brook began to speak

Sentences crept out between stones
adjectives swirled past nouns

Adverbs seeped through reeds
to stream a meaning

I couldn't understand
though the song flowed on
rising and falling like rainfall.

As I left the sound receded
quietened and then was gone.
Gone from my hearing
but there nonetheless

There to await the next traveller
with its new/ancient chatter

Hoping to be listened to
kept clean and not bled dry

lying helpless in its bed
unable to help itself
continuing its cry
repeating ….
    Look… Listen… Care…
           Look…
       Listen…
    Care…

If we don't...

If we don't make it, it doesn't matter
What matters is we tried
We took it on, we carried on
Knowing that others had lied

If we don't make it, don't look back
Don't think of our lost worlds
Our fate deserves only to be
judged by our actions and not our words

If we don't make it, remember this
We had knowledge and many chances
Not like the others on this Earth
Whose fate we took for granted

If we don't make it, it will not matter
Not even if we tried
and took it on, and carried on
ignoring those who lied

John S. Langley

The Ship

'I can fix this' the Engineer said
'See, here is my costed plan.'

'Too expensive,' said those in command
'Look, you can see that we're still afloat
We don't need to spend our money and time
on things that may never happen to this boat.'

And all onboard went along with this
They shook their heads and then they sighed
'We've still got plenty of things to do
let's hold on tight and enjoy the ride.'

'We're sinking,' said the sailor
'Sure as little fishies swim.'

'Don't bother us with this nonsense
can't you see that we're occupied
on really important matters.
Now off you go, outside.'

Said the sailor 'At least I tried.'

And all onboard went along with this
They shook their heads and then they sighed
'We've still got plenty of things to do
let's hold on tight and enjoy the ride.'

Heartwood

A passenger was getting worried
Thought she'd better have a word
But she couldn't get anyone to listen to her
became they didn't care.

'So it can't be that serious,' she thought to herself
'After all we're in the same boat
and if there was anything to worry about
they'd be sure to be on it, without doubt.'

And all aboard went along with this
They shook their heads and then they sighed
'We've still got plenty of things to do
we'll hold on tight and enjoy this ride.'

The Quartermaster said, 'The crew are restless
they can see what's beginning to happen.'
But no-one could agree on what it meant
when water was seeping in through the vent.

And all aboard started seeing this
And shook their heads and then they sighed
'There's got to be plenty that we can do
we're sure to be able to ride this tide.'

John S. Langley

The Boatswain had a message
'We'll do the best we can
although it might be too late now
look what's coming towards the bow.'

For the seventh wave had risen
And was rolling towering high

Now everyone turned and looked at this
They shook their heads and then they sighed
'Now there's nothing we can do
There are no choices left
So let's hold on tight till we finish this ride.'

And that's just what they did...

Crow Moon

The March full moon is known as the Worm Moon since this is the time of year when the ground begins to thaw and worms and insects begin to emerge. It is also known as the Sap Moon or the Crow Moon. Just a few days later astronomical Spring officially begins.

The world is on the turn
night awash
with moonshine
that be-shadows
the greys of Earth
held in restraint.

Beneath the surface
the wheel turns
and prepares to heave
wriggle
surge
unleash
it's buried colours

But for now
there is the moon
the Crow Moon
and all is still.
The world is on the turn.

John S. Langley

Shopping

Today I shall walk to the shop
and ask for a measure of milk,
a pat of butter and slices of bacon
cut particularly thick

A selection of sweets
from deep glass jars
sticky with gossip
about mothers and pa's

Then I'll walk home
on the smell of baked bread
with lots still to do
rattling round in my head.

....

Today I will drive to the shop
and trolley down the motorway
of 3 for 2's and bargains
that cannot get away

I'll buy things I need and things I don't
and people will have to get out of my way
I don't have time to be wasted
And chatting would cause a delay

Heartwood

....

Today I will go to the online shop
always open and alive and kicking
I don't ever need to move,
only my finger needs to be clicking

Delivery will be the next day
from a young man in a hurry
hitting his time slots, sweating out diesel
remembering I ordered some cherries

Then I'll rip off the plastic
from each wrapped banana
pile up the packaging
to save the Savannah

I'll pile the items into the freezer
or cupboard or into the fridge
where they can join last week's leftovers
I've over-ordered a smidge

And then I'll stop and wonder
a Ghanese coffee in my hand
at the marvel that is shopping
and the progress we have made
    all the progress
        all the progress we have made...

John S. Langley

Fire

Elemental
Lightning from above
Magma from below
Forest fires sparked
Uncontrollable
Unpredictable
Fearsome

Harnessed
Cooking our food
Heating our spaces
Lighting our way
On demand
Controlled
Conquered

Rendered
Brought into service
Domesticated
Us above animals
Proving primacy
Compliant
Docile

Heartwood

Complacency
Under-respected
Underestimated
Fuelled by ignorance
Sparking forest fires
Global warming
Viscous circle

Fierce
Wild
Hostile
Savage
Violent
Intense
... forever Elemental

John S. Langley

Embedded in Nature

I see me lying in rich dark loam among the dappled shadows
wrapped in layers of damp leaves.
I stretch out
straight back, pale arms, long legs
dig my fingers deep in yielding earth. I feel the beat of my own
heart, thub-thub, in time to the beat, thub-thub, of decay, of destruction

the thaw of regeneration.

My cells call out to earth's moisture, iron to iron, rust to rust. Rich in
calcium I dissolve, am taken in by multitudes of microbes
that swarm like mites and beetles and worm a way through soft organic
sharp mineral edges. Earth and I together. My genesis

My alpha, my omega.

***

I wake to the sound of insect's wings. The colours of autumn - reds
yellows, blacks clothe me. Mycelium veins reach for the sun's warmth.
Times pass. The first new-old sound I hear is the brown owl's 'kee-wit' ca
that splits moonlight into shards of being. I shiver in the dawn,

erect hairs stand on fresh skin laced

with an oily dew. New muscles tense, nerves fire into connection.
I am alive to the pulse of metabolic respiration
feel the balancing power of photosynthesis, and walk the
thin bio-atmospheric tightrope as a chorus chatters to

the rising light that shines above.

My unsteady step slips on a discarded plastic bag, I am
cut on the unseen sharp edge of a buried shopping trolley. There
is the sound of hooves, I see the virgin white of the Hind, leaping,

followed by a flight of arrows.

I close my eyes and the beauty dies.

***

Heartwood

Reborn: I am in a cold room with drawn curtains. I brush my teeth
in artificial white light that shines on our cleverness; plastic
toothbrush, formulated toothpaste, ceramic sink, toilet and tiles,
cotton cloths and towels, treated water on tap, hot and cold, a
silver glazed mirror gazing back

where my dream refuses to die.

I pull back the curtains, see the greyness, hear the early riser
engines rev and see, there, growing through a crack in the hardcore
a sprig of resilient green. And on a branch, on the very edge
of vision, I see a raw, red-breasted young robin
getting ready to sing.

John S. Langley

I Got the Science in Me

I am flavoured by quarks, leptons and bosons, up, down, charmed
I am strange, top to bottom. Lit by photons and built by
neutrons, protons. Orbited by electrons. My atoms
cling together in obedience to their lore of form

and cluster into molecules by practiced expertise
to form the basic building blocks: proteins, fats, nucleic
acids, carbohydrates; and onwards to the biochemical
rush of RNA, that warps and wraps and curls and seeks

an evolutionary apex: the double helix
DNA. Coding the instructions needed to construct
(and maintain for a short while) - a me or you. In each cell
nucleus the chromosomes float in cytoplasm powered

by mitochondria, mitosis, meiosis. Enclosed in thin membranes
to become bone, muscle, tendon, ligament, veins, arteries
that support and connect organs: heart, brain, kidney, liver,
lungs, spleen. Components that build systems: circulatory,

respiratory, nervous, digestion. Each one needing
to be fed; by ingested vitamins, carbohydrates,
proteins, minerals. Symbiotically dependant
on the bacteria in our guts. Held in shape by a skin that

breathes, sweats, cools, feels. A head, two arms, two legs.
Eyes, hands, feet, mouth. Sensing the external world
through sight, sound, touch, smell, and taste.

In this suit I stand. Imperfectly perfect. To speak, to
mate, to behave (well or badly). To conform (or not) to
press (or perhaps not) our innate self-destruct buttons. To
build a memory. To live, think, wonder.   Love.   Protect.

How can this be Science?

Where am I hidden, in all this?
Nurtured to make my own mistakes, memories and regret.
Where are you? Made the same. Individually unique.

So look again!

Look at the whole. This is me you can see.
Now.   Here I am.   Look.
Without even scratching the surface.

THOUGHTS AND THINGS

John S. Langley

Dinna Fergit

"Away an' wash ye-sels."
And we went to the cold tap
and splashed a little water
on our delicate, freckled, skins.

"Do ya call that washin'?
Ye'rrrl nivver git clean like that.
If aa hev te cum ove' there
I'll giv yee both a wee scrub."

We looked at each other.
We knew that she meant it so
we set to our self-cleaning
with a little more rigour.

I can still hear her voice
"Eat up ma wee scamps there's those
goin' hungry aroond the
werrrld that wud murrder fer a

meal like this … an' dinna
fergit ter eat up all yer
grrreens." I can't say every meal
was a success but we were

Heartwood

kept fed and clothed and loved.
Yes, we knew that we were cared
about. Every day. Every
minute. I met up with my

brother the other day.
We traded stories and he
asked me, "When was the last time
yer had stovies?" and when I

was slow to answer he
said, "or shell pie, tailend, neeps
tatties or a braw steamin'
clootie dumpling?". "I've travelled

a long way," I said, "let's
go and I'll get you lunch." "Aye,"
he said, "an' wash yer hands an'
dinna fergit ter eat up

all yer grrreens." It was good
to know she was still with us.

John S. Langley

Student Haunt
(Edinburgh 1970/2020)

The cafe smelt of tangerines
orange cups full of chocolate
steaming with fresh expectations
questioning the newfound known unknowns.

It was a sweaty summer then.
Marigold wore her yellow gloves
called herself enchanted with her
perfect teeth and deep dyed red hair.

When music played it was mellow
girls hip-swayed to the lavs and back
and lads took time to grow more hair
their sweaters frayed at the elbows.

Me?
     I was not there. I did not
see the talk of revolution
how we could reach up to the sky
and that would make a difference.

It was Peter who filled me in.
Three times he told me as if the
repetition could compensate
for my missing delinquent soul.

Heartwood

Those hot summers are long passed now.
The caff in a prime location
moved up-market. Selling nothing
for under a fiver.
                    But I

went back.
            Suitably dressed.
To see if the carved initials
were still there. To say sorry to
myself for missing it and to sniff

out those time-staled odours as dear
to me as the smell of fresh cut
grass, the perfume of marigolds
the still keen cost of absence.

John S. Langley

Starlight

The starlight has travelled long
to reach this glassy plain
where the light it is refracted
despite the pouring rain
and simultaneously shimmers
from the surface of a pool
is reflected, passes onwards
to seek an eye to cool.

Its natural speed with slide-rule
we arrogantly gauge
and confine it as a number
upon a frozen page.
We note it has a spectral shift
and is bent upon its path
to follow least resistance
we can calculate by math.

It is a solar system
in a tiny point of light
and falls upon a dreamer
upon a moonless night
the sleeper's eyes are shuttered
to this every-night event
with no appreciation
that this light is heaven sent.

Heartwood

It bounces from a mirror-pool
and physically unravels
caught in a watcher's eye
through iris, lens it travels
by optic nerve and evolved brain
to form a fleeting mood
then the squirrel starts and scurries
off hunting for its food.

John S. Langley

Home

Running like veins: the Land
calls us back from far places
where we silently carry
a soil so rich
that it cannot be shed

Soaring like sight: the Hills
that have nurtured and fed
our dreams with stories
of old stones, the old tales

High as the mountains
deep as the valleys
chattering like the river waters
the Land calls us back
deep rooted

Slow Down

Look in the hive

The bees can be as busy
as they like
but if there is no new brood
there is no future.

A sterile or a dead Queen
It does not
matter which

They can work as
hard as they like
bringing in pollen
dancing directions

the remaining time
can be counted in
buzzes

The colony's days are numbered

Even so they keep on
though there is no hope

Someone should tell them
to slow down
and take it easy

When there is no hope

Why rush ?

John S. Langley

Alternative Universe

The watch had stopped
Mindless neglect
and lack of attention
had run it to a halt

the hands stopped
the date frozen
to the day before
you decided to go

In the watch's Universe
there were still
23 hours
and 14 minutes left

I could not take that time away

I would get another watch

If this were real
I would still have time
to pick up the phone

to give you a call

and say all those things
and ask all those things
that in this Universe

I forgot to

Rainbows

Rays of light lie as solid as glass upon the floor
Amber sandwiched between red and green
Inspired by the sight I seek out my pen and make
Notes for future reference about this untouchable
Beam of light that even now eludes my fingertips
Observable but transient it glows and then the
Wind shifts and clouds block out the
Sun and the rainbow colours dim...
                                       ... and disappear.

John S. Langley

The Value of Work

I know what it's like
to fill the time
with work

that you hope
someone will think
is important

Because you're not sure
any more

But it fills the space
and if it wasn't there
there'd be a vacuum
and you'd be sucked into it

and spiral around
arms flailing
out of control

and that would be worse

And

And the World changes
And the Days pass
that mark,
that mark

And the World turns
And the Nights come
that sooth,
that sooth

And I will go
And I will go
When the World turns

And we will meet
And we will meet
When the Night comes

And the World will turn
And the Days will pass
And the World will change
And the Night come

To sooth
To mark
To pass

John S. Langley

And here was the Fireplace

In the centre of that wall
where the television stand is now

We used to bank it up before bed
and light it first thing
to the rasping smell of phosphorus

I remember the sharp feel of first smoke
before it got going, wisping upwards
on a good draught

then the reds and yellows, whites and blues
flickering in the flames
escaping black coal caves, weaving

shapes, making stories inside your head
giving light, giving warmth
gathering us close in Winter

to listen to the radio, toasting bread
'That darned Radio' Mum would say
'it'll be the death of conversation'

Sssh Mum, the Goons are on and
'There's a door in his pyjamas.'
But it's boarded up now

Heartwood

the chimney blocked to stop
birds getting in, crows
the noise of their flapping wings
bringing down a soot fall

Always messy to clean
taking out the ashes
and gritty, grime-filled fingernails
that emphasised the wrinkles
turning hands to hard worn skin

But that was then and this is now
sitting in the same place
that is not the same place
raking over the ashes

John S. Langley

Fire lighting

If you don't obey the rules
of fire lighting
it doesn't matter who you are
or how many fires you've lit before
spluttering and crackling comfort
into a cold night

If you don't obey the rules
each and every time
providing kindling, starting small
from a spark
nursing smoke to flame
fanning the beginnings
to a larger life

If you try to take for granted
the art of making a fire
remember that the fuel does not
know of your expertise

You must teach it again
each time
from the beginning

If you do not do this
there will be no fire

There will be no warmth
No comfort will burn
in the hearth

Heartwood

John S. Langley

Rain

You can see it coming

A dark blanket
pouring over the horizon

Smudging out the blue

Sending a chill wind
to announce its arrival

Unstoppable in its stealth

and in its silences
as it creeps forwards

shedding veils of tears

sharing its presence
as we wait for its passing

So we can wait
We can wait

for the next rain

Rainbow Autumn

The beginning of Autumn is awash with colour. On a sunny day the world glistens in gold. This short poem is based on the old school rhyme 'Richard Of York Gave Battle In Vain' that helps you remember the 7 colours of the rainbow.

Red the leaves that sing to my heart

Orange-like feathers drifting down to the earth

Yellow and crispy we pile and we kick

Green the solemn moss upon the stone wall

Blue in the sky that breaks through the grey

Indigo sits on the edges of shadows, whilst

Violet leaks in... on this beautiful day!

John S. Langley

One Among Many
Written for Remembrance Day and memories of a visit to Tyne Cot WW1 Cemetery.

                Before stones a
                rifle marks the
                place & across
                a bare strip of
                wood is written
a number, a name and all that there was time to write
So many graves, so much to do for the living who remain
to bury those that can be found, shovels to the final fight
the earth embracing those who could not stand to gain
hidden beneath, unknowing sources of our birthright
                And even now
                our eye can be
                turned, to try to
                seek and to feel
                and touch and
                and hear and
                in remembering
                let our world &
                  theirs touch
                    one more
                    time, for
                      a day

Heartwood

John S. Langley

Looking Back

The river has flowed on a century
through rapids and calms that soon will pass on
And we who would search for a memory
see vaguely at best a time that is gone

Hands we can't grasp, though we try and we fail
finding no road to a question unasked
But our hearts can beat in a synchronous trail
and words not spoken may be unmasked

Old photos can show torn ways to the soul,
and where their feet fell our own boots now go
to stones that mark places where blood can extol
in perennial petals that put on a good show

And when hail falls again on the Home windowsill
inside we'll hear bullets that reverberate still.

At the Cave Mouth

At the cave mouth
the smell of rain
the landscape softened
like a memory recalled
after too long an absence

Looking out with eyes focused on infinity
fingers matted and coated, palms smeared
in red ochre, yellow umber
ground fine from old earth
mixed, bound and blown

The cave wall behind is lit red
by the evening sun
the stone glistening with new art
not yet dry
attempting to tell a story
or leave a mark

Who now stands at the cave mouth?
The artist is gone but the art remains
the rain falls and the sky teeters
but has not yet fallen
upon our heads

John S. Langley

Worth Remembering

Entering a Hospital we become mortal
shrug off the comfortable cloak
patterned with the knowing smiles
of assurance that has always
protected us from the prospect
of endings

Those things that happen to others
with alarming regularity
but not to us

Once inside the automatic doors
close behind you so smoothly
with a whoosh and you have entered
another planet that smells of chemical
cleaners and congealed mourning
for things you'd always meant to do

These places are not devoid of joy
there are reprieves and second chances
and dedicated people who try to help
and show the better side of our nature
every minute - How do they do it?
What special gene am I missing
but is theirs?

A Hospital reminds us of our mortality
May we remember it long enough
for it to make a difference.

What's that you say?

In memory
I can still hear your voice
strong as the Robin's note

Come in and sit by my fire
while the ashes glow in the grate
And through the window
a welcome breeze

brings love instead of hate

John S. Langley

The Paying Your Dues Blues

When I feel the need to share you some blues
I got something to say boy, girl I got news
Come here young ones while my light it still lasts
Come sit at my feet and I'll tell you no lies
I'll tell ya about us an' all our strange pasts
I'll give you a hand with a word to the wise

Yea, I got the time to sing you some blues
I got stories to tell ya that'll give you some clues
Yea, while this old drum still beats I'll sing yet
It might not be much but it's the best I can get
It's my way of paying back a bit of my debt
I got tales from the past that I'll pass to you yet

Yea, you see little ones, in your eyes is the wind
Let's sail with the blues and we'll see what we find
We'll cross choppy waters but we'll not capsize
The blues they will take us across this wide tide
And though my day may draw to an end
I still have the blues with these words I can send

Yea I got the need to sing you some blues
I got something to say boy, I got some news
while I still got time to sing you the blues
I'll sing you the stories that'll help pay my dues
Yea, I'll sing you the stories
Yea, I'll sing you the blues
I'll sing you the stories
that'll help pay my dues..

Heartwood

John S. Langley

Crossings

The traffic lights are on red
I look out of the window
and see you crossing
a small hand clasped in yours

You glance up and
our eyes meet briefly.
You smile. I am so shocked
I forget to smile back.

The lights change
red-amber
then green.
I watch you cross safely

I am so sorry
I did not smile back
but now the moment is gone

Emergence

This is a poem that reflected how I was feeling at the time; the journey we'd been on and where we might be heading. I submitted it to The Cumberland News and it was printed on their Letters page in June 2021.

Surprised. Knocked off course
Miscalculation
Locked in, locked out, a new
Separation
The outside looks in. In splendid
Isolation
Within four walls we slip into a kind of
Hibernation
Virtual tools, Oh thank god for
Participation
Family matters, what is real value?
Realisation
Need for others, touch and feel
Appreciation
Fear and hope, how much rope?
Consternation
A new day, an old dawn?
Contradiction
It will be, with new words
Commence-ation
Be out. Breathe. Shout. Hug
Anticipation
A new again
Renew again
Again...

John S. Langley

Belonging

There is such beauty in a sunset
glowing orange bright
it is not easy to forget
but difficult to write

to find words that can describe the sight
moments between day and night
that make you pause and gaze
to stand and stare and raise

your head towards the sky
absorbing the colour chorus
feeling a simple oneness
a oneness with the sky

Passing Time

Passing time has never been easier.
Live TV, multiple channels, catch up
individual recordings, on demand, apps
games, email, internet, 24 hr News
social media of so many different varieties
you could make sauce out of them.

While outside, the birds sing in HD, in 3D
but cannot be paused, zoomed in on, or edited
to give the right ending, with music
and learned commentary.

This natural presentation falls short.
It is too fragmented, too uncertain.
While we crave an order that is not there.

So instead we turn to the pixelated screen
that lights up our room
and we sit and watch and hope
that our walls will stay standing.

John S. Langley

For the WI (with affection)

I was invited (with others) to present poetry to a local WI group. We were made very welcome and I hope they had as good a time as we did!

We are the WI
One for all and all for one
Meeting almost every month
Every one a joy
Never a dull moment!

Elizabeth

Evening came whether wished for or not
Like an iron hand in a velvet glove
It took away, bequeathing us only
Zigzagging queues, the silence of many
All united for a single moment
Both personal and together sharing
Everything in a look, repeating a
Thank you in silence, in flowers, for
Her life, Her reign, Her service to us all.

John S. Langley

Seeing in the Dark

You have to give it time
Get out of the street lights
car lights, house lights, security lights
and wait.

Let your colour cone receptors relax
Get your black and white rod receptors
warmed to their task.

If you must have light make it red
so as not to destroy your dark adaptation
and have to start all over again

As the darkening night starts to pop with stars
enjoy being a part of the moment
Stay quiet, let the light speak

Use binoculars or a telescope and a steady hand
Marvel at the multitude of invisible points of light
now made visible

Look for the Seven Sisters, now multiplied
Look for Orion, the blurred nebula in his belt
Look for Andromeda

Heartwood

and wonder if there are light sensitive beings
looking back.
Although as it takes 2.5million years
for the light to reach us
such a long distance relationship
would be difficult to manage

Look at the Moon
the sharp edged craters
We must have been bombarded just as severely
though the evidence has been washed away
by water, weather, and plate tectonics

And then think of what you need to do
Right here on the ground
The things you meant to do
if you had time

And in the darkness
be resolute
And before the light from your eyes
leaves Our Solar System
begin to do them.

John S. Langley

Red Squirrel

These lines were written as part of a collaboration with an artist who was hand making a print of a Red squirrel – a marvellous process to watch.

I.

Etched from ash by hand
Artist, paper, inks now one
I am made, see me

II.

Upon a branch, a moment's pause
Before I dash off on Nature's wind
Acorn and wood together bind
Me to today and winter's stores

III.

Frozen, I am art
Here I sit for all my time
Past and future fixed

IV.

Red I am and so proud to be
Acorn and tree is part of me
I'll sit and watch as my day wears on
and listen to old Nature's song

Heartwood

V.
Beech burrs burst upon the tree
Acorns fall from their cups of oak
Squirrels feed upon this bounty
And bury some for a winter store

Like forgetful gardeners they lose track
So some planted nuts then germinate
Sending forth their roots and stalks
and fight to grow for our future's sake

John S. Langley

Private Photograph

I stand in a worn blue fleece jacket
my back is towards you
my feet and legs out of sight
out of the frame

Over my shoulder and past me
the blue-grey waters of the loch
shine silver surfaced
in the diffused sunlight

that has passed through space
reached through cloud
and is reflected slant wise
to meet my eyes

that you can't see.

As you look
I start to disappear.
My grey-white hair
deranged into

the pixelated sky
not quite in focus.
My body wrapped
in pale blue mutes

Heartwood

to the whites and greys
of this sharp
winter's day

Now you can't see me.

I and the scene
are interwoven
I am it
it is me

I smile
and the light
on the loch
shivers

But you can't see that either.

John S. Langley

*'No less connected for being still
No less sentient for being silent.'*

If there's anything that's easy to take for granted then fairly close to the top of the list has got to be trees... I mean they're just there aren't they, all around us, static, and easily ignored but...

2 fully grown trees produce as much oxygen as the Carbon Dioxide a single person breathes out.

A tree consumes 48lbs (22kg) of Carbon Dioxide. The average carbon footprint of a person is 7tonnes CO2e per year - so one person needs 320 trees !

We should be planting trees not burning forests or cutting them down ...

John S. Langley

Casting Shadows

You need a strong Sun
to cast a shadow
unfogged by diffusing cloud

We may cast a long shadow
Coming and going so quickly
with so little time

to do individual harm
but collectively over time
our persistence beshadows

all that we have done, will do
with our moment in the Sun
our chance to cast a shadow

Heartwood

In Death

Spores, invisible to us
measured in micrometers
settle onto dead wood
begin to burrow
between cells
taking sustenance
hyphae creeping
massed as mycelium
suck out nutrients
secret work on the inside
break down structure
feed
build external fruiting bodies
we call brackets
ringed like the host it steals from
getting ready to dispatch
millions of spores of its own
hoping for a lucky break
a soft landing
taking its chances

Heartwood

And so the dead tree sags
rots
is home to beetles
and in death supports life
it's store of nutrients spreading
until finally it is indistinguishable
from the earth
from which it grew
it's final act to give back minerals
hard won that now
can be sought out
by the next generation
just as
in every breath we take
we inhale six molecules
of Caesar's last breath.

John S. Langley

Galaxies Collide

As up above, so it is
here down below on Earth
Galaxies collide

Not fast with fanfare
but slow and inexorable
invisible to our eye

they advance one to another
chemical, physical, biological
weapons warring at the edges

not that the heart of either
feels threatened, the distance
to the front line is too great

to affect the rhythm of its day
But it will come, it will come
inexorably... it will come

Heartwood

John S. Langley

Sunshine

Turning fields from grey to green
Bejewelling the spider's web
Silvering the barbed wire
brocaded between posts
Beaming on the butterflies
that dance in three dimensions
Creating rainbows after rain
Drying my river-splashed skin
Calming my soul
Putting the bead
in the jackdaw's beady eye.

Heartwood

John S. Langley

Sequence

I.

Each ring a resurrection
Each year a life
Forged from evolving DNA
Twisted by wind
Fed by rain
Threatened by fire
Rooted in earth

II.

Molecules absorbed, transmuted
forming forms pre-programmed
somehow knowing how to grow
capturing carbon from thin air
water sucked up from below
like blood
transporting
circulating
transferring
back and forth through
it's entire form

Heartwood

stretching out
producing structure
creating pressure
Carbon
Hydrogen
Oxygen
Minerals
all the food needed.

No need to move
all that it needs
comes to it
to nurture
and provide

And when it sheds
when it falls
it is consumed
its elements
its molecules passed
on to others
for their use.

The molecules
Carbon
Hydrogen
Oxygen
fundamentally unchanged
exchanged
forming
unforming
informing
atoms
making molecules
breaking
reforming
driven by sunlight

III.

And we, we are
fundamentally
no different

We coalesce
for a span
elemental

and then
are dispersed
as if we were
never here
or
always here
universal
émigrés
with no other home
no separation
in between ...

IV.

We all arrive
We all leave
in different forms
for differing spans
all different
all the same

Let those who can
appreciate
the warmth of the Sun

John S. Langley

of being one
amongst others
not fearing to care

There may be better ways
to arrive
There may be better ways
to depart
but we all travel
a life's journey

from the beginning
to the end
a fleeting
though conscious
part
within a greater whole.

Heartwood

John S. Langley

Skin Deep

Moss creeps onto peaks and into troughs
an outer skin exposed to the world
of frosts and winds and rain and sun
protects the insides, a tough crust
forged since birth, toughened, tempered
attacked by disease, cankered, aged
a life, a local knowledge of place
reacting to the moment, following
an imprinted path, subject to the elements
producing, shedding seeds into uncertain
tides, a species reliant on probability

I walk past you every day, ignored through
familiarity and the lack of communication
But if I pause, if I take the time to think
I realise you are older, have seen
more years, will see more years, without
you there are no me's, we each transpire
and exchange, we need each other, if we
remove you it is like cutting out our own
lungs, you have no defence to our metal
onslaught ... I hope we will re-learn
a mutual respect.

Heartwood

John S. Langley

Differences

Different types of bark
Different heights
Different canopies
Different leaves
Different fruits and flowers
Different seeding
Different locations
Some deciduous
Some evergreen
Existing together
Existing apart
Evolving
Can they teach us?
Can we learn?

Leaf Blowing

Do you know how much a leaf blower costs?
Or how many hours I spend
clearing up your mess?
Of course you don't.
You just do the same thing
every year.
Thoughtlessly divesting yourself
of redundant leaves.
Shedding them
in a blaze of glory
all around!
Why do you not shed them in neat piles?
It would make my life so much easier.
You would have thought
after all these years
you would have learned.
Or is it me?

John S. Langley

Storm Struck

Did you feel any pain?
When you were storm struck
When the flash of intense light
(that you did not see)
cracked from the sky and struck
your outstretched limb, severing
and cauterising as you became
it's milliseconds route to earth
leaving behind no memory
save the roll of thunder
(that you did not hear)
the blocked road and the scorched
black scarred stump that smoked
and sizzled for a short time
before being quenched by the heavy rain.

But you did feel the change in balance
the pull on your roots, the new motion
in the wind.

Lucky for you your roots ran deep
with arms and fingers and capillary hairs
embedded in a rich soil that clung and held.

Heartwood

Over the years I have watched as your wound
has weathered into a part of you, as you
have grown new limbs, as you have learned
to lean and take on a new grown balance
a new equilibrium.

Since that night
you have withstood many storms.

The road was cleared quickly
your shed limb sawn, shredded
and part stored
to be cremated
in an open hearth.

What do you know of all this?
You keep your history close
locked away.

If you speak
I do not hear
there is so much
I do not see.

John S. Langley

Fallen

Storm Arwen took you down
(a name we gave it)
A 100mph gust amidst the gale
(a measure we gave it)
Was too much for your shallow roots
your high centre of gravity
(an explanation we gave it)
And you fell
(you felt it)

And we fell upon your carcass
with chainsaws and shredders we began
to move your body from where
we did not want it to be.
Too close to beehives
too unstable for grandchildren.

Inside you kept your story, a hidden library
tucked away like old photographs in a bottom drawer
until we sliced through it, again and again
unlocked by a force stronger than any storm
the rings of your history, the thin years of drought
the years of warmth and sun and rain
the concentric cycles of your being
from the first sprouting to your catastrophic end

Heartwood

We shredded the small stuff, burnt the branches
stacked the logs to dry and left the stump.

Now a year later we warm ourselves by your history
and you are reborn!
Sprouting fresh stalks from your stump
a fresh start and we unsure
about what happens next!

John S. Langley

Rings

Our named seasons mean nothing to you
We count time in segments while you
live a continuum sensing through your
fibre the change in temperature
the balance between light and dark
that tells you the time to bud, to leaf
and give birth in your core to a new ring
that through moisture and pressure
takes its place, pushing out
the circumference
deepening the crevices in your
cracked and crinkled bark.

...

And if I listen
if I put my ear to your skin
I can hear
the creak and squeak
of your growth
the whoosh and gurgle
of your circulation.

Heartwood

...

And later this same alchemy
brings the discarding
of sugar producing leaves
the loss of resources
to protect the core
and to maintain
and cool
and wait
for the next reincarnation
the next ring.

John S. Langley

Utility

Owls nest and use the height
to hoot out across the darkest night
looking down for signs of movement

The mottled Treecreeper dons it's
invisibility pressed down into crevices
keeping silent, still ... and safe

Those holes sunk deep by the hammering
head of a concussion-proof woodpecker
are a sounding board, a signal, a refuge

Flocks of small birds passing through
chirp and flash red, blue, yellow as they flit
not still, always moving, always wary

Rooks peruse with a mean eye while
Jackdaws spy out opportunities and
in winter the Fieldfare flock

Insects, fungi, and our lungs; one tree
so many guests, unwanted or welcome
one world within a world ... one tree

Green Man

Face on a felled tree
Head of leaves, eyes of heartwood
Asks what we're doing

John S. Langley

HADRIAN's WALL 1900

In 2022, to celebrate the 1900th anniversary of the beginning of the construction of Hadrian's Wall, a community arts project was run using the what3words app (that gives a unique three word designation to each 3m square space in the UK – and beyond) to inspire poetry and art around the Lanercost to Birdoswald section of the Wall. Local community groups, schools and individuals were all involved and the project culminated in an exhibition in the Brampton Community Centre. The following are slightly revised versions of my submissions to the project.

John S. Langley

Birdoswald Fort
(emperor.inflamed.curl)

At the Gate I stand
just another guard duty
At my back the Empire
and the smell of horses.

In front of me is the town
always so busy
Full of hustle and heaving
the sound of voices
Subdued or inflamed
differing tongues and accents
Steaming the cold air.

I curl up in my woollen cloak
bought by good sense
and a fine win at dice.
I know I am not built
for these foreign climes
but I have a job to do.
Here, a stranger approaches
"Quo vadis,
wither goest thou?"

Heartwood

John S. Langley

Turret 51a - Piper Sike
(keys.approvals.scared)

They built me out of stone you know
Approved by order from the top.
I was first keyed into a cheap turf Wall
but always stood here strong and tall.

The old turf just got full of weeds
and creepy-crawlies through and through
so they rebuilt it in good stone and
Candidus* was pleased with what he'd done

I might not be much to look at now
but think on. I was important once!

* A stone found 128m from the Turret had
an inscription which, roughly translated,
recorded 'the century of Candidus Creocens
... built this stretch of wall.'

Heartwood

John S. Langley

Turret 51b – Leahill
(impose.snuggled.halt)

Put another log on the fire
will you Linus
warm up the stew and pass me
some of that fresh bread.
It's bitter outside
but I've cleared away
most of the snow.

These night shifts aren't funny
but they've got to be done.
It's your turn now Marcus
so off you go, quick, quick.
It's all quiet now
after our Summer troubles.

The moon is bright.
I'd keep moving if I were you
and stamp your feet.
Now it's my turn to get some sleep.

Heartwood

John S. Langley

Banks East Turret
(gladiator.tolerates.spoils)

I'm far from the arena
- thank goodness.

Being a slave isn't so bad
- sometimes.

At least here there's a great view
- the wrong way!

Out over the friendly side
to the South.

You have to be up top
to see the North.
But that's not me.
I work at ground level
doing these Romans' dirty work
clearing latrines
stoking fires
all day long.

But I eat
and keep out of trouble
I do what I'm told
- it's safer that way!

Heartwood

John S. Langley

Lanercost Priory
(stones.guesswork.wagers)

Roman Altar Stone
(Standing on display in the crypt of Lanercost Priory)

So there I was
formed over several eons
lying underground
minding my own business
when I was disturbed
by this iron hammering
that split me from the rest
lifted and chiselled me
into something
you creatures worshipped
pouring oil
laying gifts.

For hundreds of years
I was honoured
until it collapsed
around me
and I returned
to the soil
content to remain there.

But again
I was uncovered
stood in a crypt
to be gawped at.

When will you people ever leave me alone!?

Heartwood

John S. Langley

Remember the Best Bits

I know I could be cantankerous
grouchy and irritating too
But what I'd like you to do
is remember some of the best bits.

It's easy to remember the frailty
of the last days and the last time
But it really isn't a crime
to also remember the best bits

There were some you know
plenty to raise a laugh or a smile
Nice to pause and think for a while
of some of the best bits

The best bits are what I'd prefer
that people choose to recall
if I'm remembered at all
...and that would be one of the best bits

Aye, that would be one of the best bits

Heartwood

www.ingramcontent.com/pod-product-compliance
Lightning Source LLC
Chambersburg PA
CBHW030039100526
44590CB00011B/262